WHEN CRABS CROSS THE SAND

THE CHRISTMAS ISLAND CRAB MIGRATION

BY SHARON KATZ COOPER

ILLUSTRATED BY CHRISTINA WALD

raintree

a Capstone company — publishers for children

Raintree is an imprint of Capstone Global Library Limited, a company incorporated in England and Wales having its registered office at 7 Pilgrim Street, London, EC4V 6LB – Registered company number: 6695582

www.raintree.co.uk
myorders@raintree.co.uk

With thanks to our advisers for their expertise, research and advice:

Elizabeth Davis-Berg, PhD, Associate Professor of Biology
Columbia College Chicago, USA

Terry Flaherty, PhD, Professor of English
Minnesota State University, Mankato, USA

Editorial Credits
Jill Kalz, editor; Lori Bye, designer; Nathan Gassman, art director; Laura Manthe, production specialist

ISBN 978 1 4747 6466 7
21..20..19..18 17
10 9 8 7 6 5 4 3 2 1

British Library Cataloguing in Publication Data
A full catalogue record for this book is available from the British Library.

Photo Credits
The illustrations in this book were created with acrylics.
Image Credit: Shutterstock: pavalena, 3 (map)

Every effort has been made to contact copyright holders of material reproduced in this book. Any omissions will be rectified in subsequent printings if notice is given to the publisher.

All the Internet addresses (URLs) given in this book were valid at the time of going to press. However, due to the dynamic nature of the Internet, some addresses may have changed, or sites may have changed or ceased to exist since publication. While the author and publisher regret any inconvenience this may cause readers, no responsibility for any such changes can be accepted by either the author or the publisher.

Printed and bound in India.

On Christmas Island, red crabs act like any other land crabs for most of the year. They live quietly in burrows dug into the forest floor. But once a year, millions of them migrate towards the Indian Ocean. The whole island turns bright red. For several weeks, crabs climb across, over and down anything in their path to reach the beach. Why is this journey so important to them?

Drip, drop! Drip, drop! The sound of rain wakes up the red crab. She stretches and waves her claws. She hasn't moved for a long time. During the dry winter months, she slept, tucked safe inside her moist burrow.

Now the rainy season begins. The red crab clears the opening to her burrow. *Scuttle!* Another red crab almost steps on her. *Scuttle! Scuttle!* Dozens of red crabs skitter by. They are all walking in the same direction. They are heading towards the beach.

The red crab feels the need to follow them. The beach is far away for an animal her size. The long, dangerous journey will take more than one week.

Along the way she climbs over rocks and fallen trees. She stops to eat leaves and seeds. She crosses roads and just misses being hit by a car.

The red crab comes to a steep cliff. But it does not stop her. She climbs down quickly. Thousands upon thousands of crabs crawl with her.

The crabs have been walking for just over one week. The air outside the forest is drier than inside their burrows. They need to stay wet or they will die. Where is the beach?

There it is! The Indian Ocean! The red crab scurries in.

After a dip in the water, the red crab walks back up the beach. Quick as a blink, two claws grab her. It's a male crab. He arrived first to get his beach burrow ready for her. The two crabs crawl inside the burrow and mate. Once they've mated the male goes back into the forest. The female stays behind. She has important work to do.

The red crab watches the moon. She watches the tide. When the time is right, she leaves the sandy burrow and runs to the water. Raising her claws above her, she does a little dance. She shakes her body up and down to drop thousands of eggs into the ocean. Hundreds of other female red crabs do the same thing.

As soon as the red crab's eggs hit the water, two things happen. Firstly, her job is done. The red crab goes back to the forest the same way she came. Secondly, all the eggs hatch! Millions of tiny crab larvae swirl around in the water. Crab babies must hatch in sea water. This explains why the red crabs must make such long journeys.

The larvae grow in the ocean for about one month. Fish gobble up many of them. The lucky larvae change into tiny baby crabs no bigger than pencil erasers. They leave the ocean by the millions and turn the whole water's edge red.

The tiny red crabs scramble towards the forest. No one tells them where to go. They just know. They will spend the next four or five years hiding between rocks and under leaves.

Then they too will take part in the amazing red crab migration.

Christmas Island Crab Fast Facts

Scientific name: *Gecarcoidea natalis*

Adult size (about 4 to 5 years old): carapace roughly 11 centimetres (4.5 inches) wide

Home: Christmas Island, a territory of Australia, off the northwestern coast of Australia, near the equator

Eggs: females lay up to 100,000 eggs at a time; egg-laying happens before the morning of the high tide that comes before the December new moon

Diet: fallen leaves, seeds, fruit, snails, dead animals, human rubbish

Life span: roughly 20 to 30 years

Natural predators: none on Christmas Island; young are eaten by fish and other animals in the sea

Main threat: climate change; Christmas Island crabs will not migrate or mate if too little rain falls, putting them in danger of dying out

Migration: around 50 million crabs take part; the only species of land crabs where both males and females migrate

Comprehension Questions

1. Why is it important for millions of Christmas Island crabs to go to the beach every year?

2. Describe the dangers Christmas Island crabs face on their migration journey.

3. What does the pull-out image on page 18 show? Why does the illustrator use a pull-out here?

Glossary

burrow tunnel or hole in the ground made or used by an animal to live in

carapace hard shell that covers the main part of a crab's body

climate average weather conditions of a place throughout the year

equator imaginary line around the middle of Earth

high tide when the sea reaches its highest level on land

larva stage in development between an egg and an adult; the word for more than one larva is "larvae"

mate join together to produce young; a mate is also the male or female partner of a pair of animals

migrate move from one area to another on a regular basis, usually to find food or to produce young

tide regular rising and falling of the sea, which usually happens twice a day

Read More

Amazing Animal Journeys (Great Migrations), Laura Marsh (National Geographic Society, 2010)

Hermit Crabs (Keeping Unusual Pets), Tristan Boyer Binns (Heinemann Library, 2011)

Why Do Crabs Walk Sideways (Seashore Life), Anna Claybourne (Miles Kelly Publishing, 2012)

Websites

www.bbc.co.uk/nature/life/Malacostraca
Search the BBC nature website to find out all the latest news about crabs from all over the world.

www.christmas.net.au/experiences/red-crab-migration
Discover all the details of the Christmas Island red crab migration on this website.

www.education.nationalgeographic.com/education/media/crab-den
Even more fascinating facts and interesting video clips about red crab migrations can be found on the National Geographic website.

Index

LOOK OUT FOR ALL THE BOOKS IN THE SERIES:

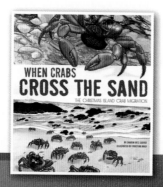
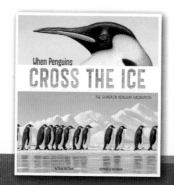
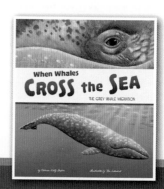